Mike Lowell

and the BOSTON RED SOX

2007 WORLD SERIES

by Michael Sandler

Consultant: Jim Sherman
Head Baseball Coach
University of Delaware

BEARPORT
PUBLISHING

New York, New York

Credits

Cover and Title Page, © Jaime Squire/Getty Images; 4, © Boston Globe/Stan Grossfeld/ Landov; 5, © Robert Caplin/Bloomberg News/Landov; 7, © David Bergman/Corbis; 8, © George Rizov; 9, Courtesy FIU Athletic Media Relations, Florida International University; 10, © Scott Halleran/Allsport/Getty Images; 12, © Barry Taylor/Ai Wire/ Newscom.com; 13, © Ezra Shaw/Getty Images; 14, © REUTERS/Shaun Best; 15, © Brad Mangin/MLB Photos via Getty Images; 16, © Brian Snyder/Reuters/Landov; 17, © Elsa/ Getty Images; 18, © Ron Vesely/MLB Photos via Getty Images; 19, © REUTERS/Mike Segar; 20, © Ron Vesely/MLB Photos via Getty Images; 21, © Paul Buck/epa/Corbis; 22T, © Elsa/Getty Images; 22C, © Elsa/Getty Images; 22B, © REUTERS/Ron Kuntz.

Publisher: Kenn Goin
Senior Editor: Lisa Wiseman
Creative Director: Spencer Brinker
Design: Stacey May
Photo Researcher: James O'Connor

Library of Congress Cataloging-in-Publication Data
Sandler, Michael, 1965-
Mike Lowell and the Boston Red Sox : 2007 World Series / by Michael Sandler
consultant, Jim Sherman.
   p. cm. — (World Series superstars)
 Includes bibliographical references and index.
 ISBN-13: 978-1-59716-739-0 (library binding)
 ISBN-10: 1-59716-739-8 (library binding)
1. Lowell, Mike—Juvenile literature. 2. Baseball players—United States—
Biography—Juvenile literature. 3. Boston Red Sox (Baseball team) —Juvenile
literature. 4. World Series (Baseball) (2007) —Juvenile literature. I. Sherman, Jim. II.
Title.

 GV865.L69S36 2009
 796.357092—dc22
 (B)
                          2008001995

For more information, write to Bearport Publishing Company, Inc., 101 Fifth Avenue, Suite 6R, New York, New York 10003. Printed in the United States of America.

10 9 8 7 6 5 4 3 2 1

★ Contents ★

On a Mission

Since **opening day**, the Boston Red Sox had one goal—winning the 2007 World Series! Now the Red Sox were finally close to achieving it. They had beaten the Colorado Rockies in three straight World Series games. One more win and the **title** was theirs.

Third baseman Mike Lowell had helped Boston win games all season. Now, in the year's most important game, he was ready to do it again.

Boston fans make themselves at home at Coors Field in Denver, Colorado.

Mike Lowell

In 2007, Mike Lowell had **career highs** in hits, batting average, and **RBIs**.

Learning the Game

Mike was born in Puerto Rico but grew up in Coral Gables, Florida. He learned to play baseball from his father, Carl, who had once been a pitcher for the Puerto Rican national baseball team.

As a child, Mike's favorite day was Wednesday. On that day, his dad, a dentist, would take off from work. He'd bring Mike and his brother, Carlos, to the ball field. There they would practice batting for hours.

Mike was born in San Juan, the capital of Puerto Rico.

A baseball stadium in
San Juan, Puerto Rico

Carl Lowell was Mike's
coach throughout his
Little League career.

Getting Stronger

Mike became a very skilled **infielder**. The only problem was his size. Mike was short and very skinny. His high school coach told him he had to get stronger.

This was all that Mike needed to hear. He began lifting weights in a friend's garage four times a week. Soon he was bigger and became one of the team's best players. After high school, he went on to play baseball for Florida International University.

To get more playing time, Mike transferred to Coral Gables Senior High School in his junior year.

Mike playing baseball for Florida International University

Mike played second base and shortstop in high school and in college.

Shocking News

In 1995, Mike was **drafted** by the New York Yankees. After a few years with New York's **minor-league** teams, the Yankees traded him to the Florida Marlins.

Mike was surprised, but a bigger shock came a few weeks later. During the Marlins' training camp, he went for a **physical exam**. There, the doctor gave him some terrible news.

"Mike," he said, "you've got **cancer**."

Mike was terrified. He was only 24 years old.

The Yankees moved Mike to third base. He has played that position ever since.

Mike's 1999
Florida Marlins
baseball card

Mike was traded to the Florida
Marlins on February 1, 1999.

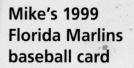

Bouncing Back

Mike was lucky. He was able to beat the disease after weeks of **radiation treatments**. Three months later, he was back playing baseball.

At first it was tough. The treatments that let him live also stole his strength and skills. Mike worked hard to get them back.

Each year he got better and better. He even played in three **All-Star Games** and helped Florida win the 2003 World Series.

Mike being introduced before the start of the 2002 All-Star Game

Mike (top) celebrates with his team after winning the 2003 World Series.

Who did Florida beat in the 2003 World Series? Mike's old team—the New York Yankees!

Batting for Boston

Before the 2006 season began, Mike was traded to the Boston Red Sox. He was excited to join the team. The Red Sox were a powerful group led by **sluggers** such as Manny Ramirez and David Ortiz.

Back in 2004, Boston had won the World Series. Mike hoped to get them there again. Sadly, neither he nor the team had a very good year. By August, the Red Sox were out of the **playoff race**.

In 2006, David Ortiz set the Red Sox record for home runs with 54.

Mike fields the ball for his new team, the Boston Red Sox.

After the 2005 season, Mike was awarded a **Gold Glove** for his excellent fielding.

The 2007 Team

The next year was a different story for the team. In the 2007 lineup, Mike batted after David Ortiz and Manny Ramirez. Pitchers often **intentionally walked** these two players. They didn't want them hitting home runs.

Mike hit so well, however, that pitchers couldn't throw walks to David and Manny. If they did, they risked Mike getting a hit and sending the two sluggers home.

Boston scored lots of runs and won many games in 2007. In the playoffs, they beat the Los Angeles Angels and the Cleveland Indians to reach the World Series.

David Ortiz (left) and Manny Ramirez (right) helped Boston beat the Los Angeles Angels in the first round of the playoffs.

Boston lost three of the first four games against Cleveland. They came back, however, to win the series.

In 2007, Mike had the fifth-highest **batting average** in the **American League**.

The Colorado Rockies

In the 2007 World Series, Boston faced the Colorado Rockies. Colorado was baseball's hottest team.

In Game 1 at Boston's Fenway Park, starter Josh Beckett cooled the Rockies down. He allowed just one run for a Red Sox win. Then Boston took Game 2 as well. Mike's fifth-inning double knocked home the winning run.

In Denver for Game 3, the results were the same. Boston destroyed Colorado, 10-5. Now Boston was just one win away from the title.

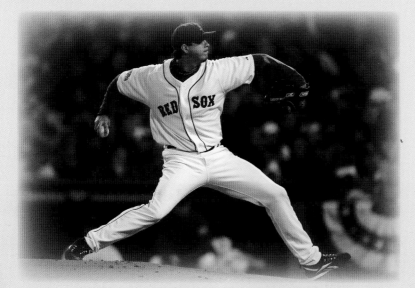

Pitcher Josh Beckett during Game 1

Mike hits a double against the Rockies in Game 2.

Before facing Boston, Colorado had lost just once in their last 22 games.

Game Four

The Red Sox were determined to achieve their season-long goal with a Game 4 win. On the **mound**, Jon Lester pitched over five scoreless innings. Could Boston's hitters do their part, too?

The answer was yes. David Ortiz knocked in a first-inning run. In the fifth inning, Mike doubled and scored. Then he led off the seventh with a booming home run. In the eighth, teammate Bobby Kielty hit another.

Boston held on for a 4-3 victory. Mike and the Red Sox were champions!

Mike (right) makes his way to home plate after hitting a home run in Game 4.

Mike was named Most Valuable Player (MVP) of the 2007 World Series.

21

Mike, along with some other key players, helped the Boston Red Sox win the 2007 World Series.

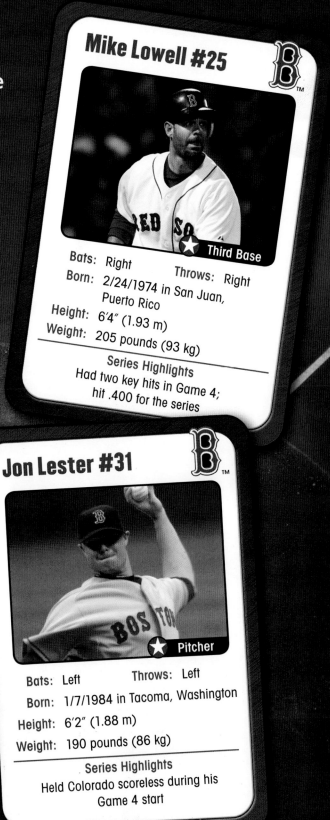

Mike Lowell #25

Third Base

Bats: Right   Throws: Right
Born: 2/24/1974 in San Juan, Puerto Rico
Height: 6'4" (1.93 m)
Weight: 205 pounds (93 kg)

Series Highlights
Had two key hits in Game 4; hit .400 for the series

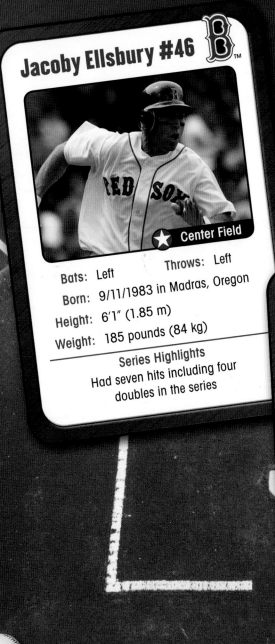

Jacoby Ellsbury #46

Center Field

Bats: Left   Throws: Left
Born: 9/11/1983 in Madras, Oregon
Height: 6'1" (1.85 m)
Weight: 185 pounds (84 kg)

Series Highlights
Had seven hits including four doubles in the series

Jon Lester #31

Pitcher

Bats: Left   Throws: Left
Born: 1/7/1984 in Tacoma, Washington
Height: 6'2" (1.88 m)
Weight: 190 pounds (86 kg)

Series Highlights
Held Colorado scoreless during his Game 4 start

Glossary

All-Star Games (AWL-STAR GAMEZ) games played between the American and National Leagues; only the best players in each league get to play

American League (uh-MER-uh-kuhn LEEG) one of the two major professional baseball leagues in the United States

batting average (BAT-ing AV-uh-rij) a statistic that measures a player's ability to get hits

cancer (KAN-sur) a serious, often deadly disease

career highs (kuh-RIHR HYEZ) personal records; the best a player has ever achieved

drafted (DRAFT-id) picked to play for a professional team

Gold Glove (GOHLD GLUHV) an award given to a player for his outstanding fielding skills

infielder (IN-feel-dur) a person who plays at either first base, second base, third base, or shortstop

intentionally walked (in-TEN-shuh-nul-ee WAWKT) a player sent to first base after a pitcher throws four balls on purpose

minor league (MYE-nur LEEG) baseball teams run by the major-league teams that are used to train young players

mound (MOUND) a small hill on the baseball field where the pitcher stands to throw the ball

opening day (OH-puh-ning DAY) the first game of a new baseball season

physical exam (FIZ-uh-kuhl eg-ZAM) a checkup performed by a doctor to evaluate a person's overall health

playoff race (PLAY-awf RAYSS) the competition, during the regular season, to have the best record and earn a spot in the playoffs

radiation treatments (*ray*-dee-AY-shuhn TREET-ments) medical remedies often used to treat cancer

RBIs (AR-BEE-EYEZ) runs batted in; at bats that bring other players, already on base, in to score

sluggers (SLUHG-erz) players who often hit doubles, triples, and home runs

title (TYE-tuhl) the championship; in baseball, a World Series win

Bibliography

Bamberger, Michael. "A Swing and a Prayer." *Sports Illustrated* (May 27, 2002).

Cafardo, Nick. "A Firm Foundation at Third." *Baseball Digest* (June 1, 2007).

Edes, Gordon. "Just Another Comeback Year." *The Boston Globe* (January 12, 2006).

Minichino, Adam. "Lowell Fighting Cancer Battle One Day at a Time." *Athens Banner-Herald* (June 9, 1999).

Read More

Nichols, John. *The Story of the Boston Red Sox.* Mankato, MN: Creative Education (2007).

Sandler, Michael. *Manny Ramirez and the Boston Red Sox: 2004 World Series.* New York: Bearport Publishing (2008).

Learn More Online

To learn more about Mike Lowell,
the Boston Red Sox, and the World Series, visit
www.bearportpublishing.com/WorldSeriesSuperstars

Index